The Book of
Country Music Wisdom

The Book of
Country Music Wisdom

Common Sense and Uncommon Genius
From 101 Country Music Greats

Compiled and Edited by Criswell Freeman

WALNUT GROVE PRESS
Nashville, TN 37211

ISBN 0-9640955-1-3

The ideas expressed in this book are not, in all cases, exact quotations, as some have been edited for clarity and brevity. In all cases, the author has attempted to maintain the speaker's original intent. In some cases, material for this book was obtained from secondary sources, primarily print media. While every effort was made to ensure the accuracy of these sources, the accuracy cannot be guaranteed. For additions, deletions, corrections or clarifications in future editions of this text, please write WALNUT GROVE PRESS.

Fourth Printing
Printed in the United States of America
Typesetting & Page Layout by Sue Gerdes
4 5 6 7 8 9 10 • 99 00 01 02 03

ACKNOWLEDGMENTS

The author wishes to acknowledge the generosity of the staff of the Country Music Foundation. The able assistance of the men and women of the Nashville Public Libraries is also recognized. The author gratefully acknowledges the helpful support of June Bowen, Angela Freeman, Mary Freeman, Mary Jo Freeman, J.R. Freeman, Hal May, Dan Mazer, Steve Parker, Don Pippen, Ronnie Pugh, Bette Schnitzer and George Schnitzer.

Finally, the author wishes to thank the countless men and women who, for over fifty years, have documented the history of country music. Without their work, this text would have been impossible.

In Memory of My Grandfather,
Harvey Freeman

Table of Contents

Introduction

This book came into existence almost by accident. While searching for ideas to round out a text on American wisdom, I decided to add a few thoughts from country music notables. I picked up the phone, called the Country Music Foundation in Nashville, Tennessee, and made an appointment to visit their archives. Upon arrival, I was handed a stack of books, and I began reading.

The words of such country legends as Hank Williams and Minnie Pearl almost jumped off the page. These were not spoiled superstars, nor were they naive dreamers. They were hard-working people who knew about life's ups and downs through personal experiences. By the end of my first afternoon in the archives, I was convinced that this book should be written.

I began visiting libraries, poring over hundreds of old magazines, books, biographies, and newspaper articles. With each passing day, I gained more and more respect for the people who make the music. Their stories are testimonies to faith, hope and optimism.

I have attempted to craft this book like a country song: memorable, powerful, and to the point. In describing a good song, Don Williams once observed, "The most significant thing any of us can do is put the message in today's language, so that it strikes a chord." I hope you enjoy these words of wisdom, and I hope they strike a chord within your heart — just like a good country song.

1

All-Purpose Advice

Whether it's the timeless verse of Hank Williams or the earthy humor of Minnie Pearl, country music spins a tale of life, love, heartache and hope — a thread of wisdom is woven throughout. The men and women who make the music have much to say about the ups and downs of everyday living. The rest of us are well advised to listen carefully.

In this chapter, we consider a country-sized helping of helpful advice. Help yourself. And then pass it on along!

See with your heart.

Ronnie Milsap

Take the back roads instead of the highways.

Minnie Pearl

Don't be afraid to fall flat on your face.

Eddy Arnold

My personal philosophy is simple:
Never limit yourself.

Dwight Yoakam

Every day, do something *you* want to do.

Doug Stone

Don't ever be afraid to fight for something
worth fighting for.

Garth Brooks

Keep your words soft and sweet. You never know when you might have to eat them.

Jerry Clower

Leave something good in every day.

Dolly Parton

The best advice my mother ever gave me was simple: She said don't forget to say your prayers.

Lorrie Morgan

Play in tune, play in good taste, and be nice to people.

Chet Adkins

If I'm having a problem with someone, I tell them. And if I love someone, I tell them.

Faith Hill

Be rude to no one.

George Morgan

Be true to your own music.

Alan Jackson

Dig down deep inside your heart and find
what's right.

Waylon Jennings

Just keep taking chances and having fun.

Garth Brooks

Believe in yourself. Work hard.
Keep your sense of humor. And one more
thing: Keep your day job.

Dolly Parton

You're no value to someone else until you're valuable to yourself.

Don Light

Don't pay interest. If you can't afford it,
don't buy it.

Webb Pierce

Don't lend money.

Eddy Arnold

I don't owe one man one cent. Anywhere.

Roy Acuff

Make sure your diamond is as polished
as it can be.

Sonny Throckmorton

Don't be afraid to give up the good
to go for the great.

Kenny Rogers

Listen to advice, but follow your heart.

Conway Twitty

If you want to grow, be open to criticism.

Kathy Mattea

Always be "work in progress."

Tim DuBois

Read with reckless abandon.

Don Schlitz

Live clean, work hard, and don't fudge.

Sonny Throckmorton

I don't have unattainable goals. I just want to be a better person. I found out the better I am, the happier I am.

Johnny Cash

Don't trust lust.

Paul Overstreet

2

Country Music

In the early days of the Grand Ole Opry, the master of ceremonies, George D. Hay, instructed entertainers to "Keep it close to the ground, boys." He wanted performers to remain true to their rural roots. The Opry stars followed Mr. Hay's advice and the rest, of course, is country music history.

This chapter contains a collection of earthy thoughts from men and women who have stayed very close to the ground. On the following pages, we pause to consider a musical style that moves both the feet and the heart, but not necessarily in that order.

F or the past hour you have been listening
to the grand opera; now we bring you
"The Grand Ole Opry."

George D. Hay

"The Solemn Ol' Judge" was the original host of the "Tennessee Barn
Dance" radio program. After he made this impromptu remark on the air,
the name of the show was forever changed to
"The Grand Ole Opry."

I n the old days, it was called "hillbilly music";
but if you called somebody a hillbilly, you were
making fun of him. Hillbilly meant inferior.
I started telling record companies, "Let's not
call it hillbilly; let's call it something else" —
and I thought, "Why not call it 'country?'"
The name stuck. Nobody calls it
hillbilly music anymore.

Ernest Tubb

Tubb is recognized for popularizing the name "country music."

I started in rock music and worked my way up to country.

Conway Twitty

The Opry is everything to me.
It's the pinnacle.

Garth Brooks

If you talk bad about country music,
it's like saying bad things about my momma.
Them's fightin' words.

Dolly Parton

I don't know what you mean by country music.
I just make music the way I know how.

Hank Williams, Sr.

Country music was always an influence
on my kind of music.

Elvis Presley

A good country song taps into strong undercurrents of family, faith and patriotism.

George Bush

Country music springs from the heart of America.

Tex Ritter

Country music belongs to America.

Bill Monroe

There's more than one kind of country music.

Pam Tillis

There are two things I won't argue about, because you can't change peoples' minds. One is the Bible. The other is country music.

Ralph Emery

A good country song takes a page out of somebody's life and puts it to music.

Conway Twitty

Country music is about the things we all face — no matter who you are or where you come from. It's about love and life. Timeless topics are the roots of country music.

Radney Foster

True country music is honesty, sincerity, and real life to the hilt.

Garth Brooks

Country music is a state of mind.

Clint Black

The poetry of country music will survive.

Rodney Crowell

Bluegrass is
wonderful music.
I'm glad I originated it.

Bill Monroe

Music is not just my passion —
it's my companion.

Ronnie Milsap

I'm proud that I was in the business during
the beautiful, golden days of country music.

Porter Wagoner

An old piano, which I learned to play by ear,
became an inseparable companion.

Floyd Cramer

I grew up in old Nashville. I know what
real country music is…and I love it.

Pam Tillis

I'm not leaving country music —
I'm taking it with me.

Dolly Parton

3

Success

Country entertainers work hard to achieve success. Theirs is not a business of forty-hour weeks or paid vacations. To the contrary, the music business can be a grinding way of life. Still, for those who truly love the music, it's the greatest profession in the world.

In the business of music, overnight stardom is the rare exception; the climb to the top usually takes many years. This long struggle gives most country stars plenty of time to reflect upon the ingredients of success. Here are some things they've learned along the way.

Success, we must remember, is in the eye of the beholder.

Tennessee Ernie Ford

Success is being happy with yourself,
having good health, and doing
what you want to do.

Billy Joe Royal

If you're dedicated, if it's something that
lives and breathes in your heart, then
you've simply got to go ahead and do it.

Rodney Crowell

Life, in general, is picking something
to strive for, and then when you get that,
picking something else.

Doug Stone

The only thing that stops you is yourself.
Period.

Sammy Kershaw

You are only as limited as you want to be.
So don't limit yourself.

Shania Twain

You paint your own future.

Eddie Rabbitt

In the long run, you make your own luck —
good, bad, or indifferent.

Loretta Lynn

If you don't like the road you're walking,
start paving another one.

Dolly Parton

You can't wait
on success.

Alan Jackson

Put the dime in the slot yourself.
    If you're not satisfied with life,
        do something about it yourself.

Mel Tillis

Don't worry about trying to be like
everybody else. Don't worry about "fitting in."
    Just be honest and do it your way.

Garth Brooks

Do what needs doin'.

Pam Tillis

Self-pity is bull.

Hank Williams, Jr.

Do you want to be successful?
Nurture your talent.

Tennessee Ernie Ford

Keep learning, keep doing, and get your ducks in a row. Then, when opportunity knocks, you're ready.

Buck Owens

If you really want something, make prepartions and pay the price.

Dolly Parton

The best advice I can give is to know *exactly* what you're going to do when you get your big break.

Terri Clark

Try, but don't try too hard. Just try hard
enough, and things will go better.

Rodney Crowell

It is important for me to try, and having tried
I look back on failure and success
as if it were all the same.

Tom T. Hall

You'll never do a whole lot unless you're
brave enough to try.

Dolly Parton

Trying is what counts.

Marty Robbins

The secret of success is
being willing to jump in
and face the fear
of failure.

Trisha Yearwood

Control success before it controls you.

Dwight Yoakam

4

Tough Times

There's an old joke that goes something like:

Question: "What do you get when you play a country record backwards?"

Answer: "You get your sweetheart back, you get your dog back, and you get your truck back."

Country music doesn't shy away from heartache or hard times. Maybe that's because stars are so familiar with the subject matter.

Country has its roots in hardship and struggle; but we should never confuse difficult circumstances with poverty of spirit. Character is often forged in the furnace of adversity.

I was *blessed* with humble beginnings.

Dolly Parton

We were so poor that is was the 40's before
we knew there had been a Depression.

Chet Atkins

Being poor really helped me.

Loretta Lynn

One of the greatest gifts a person can have —
and this is going to sound really strange —
is to be born poor.

Naomi Judd

The proverbial
wolf at the door
had a litter of pups
on my back porch.

Red Foley

I'll always be poor in my mind.

Chet Atkins

Once you've been poor, you always feel
in the back of your mind that
you'll be poor again.

Loretta Lynn

Growin' up, we had runnin' water
when we'd run and get it.

Dolly Parton

What keeps me going? The fear of starving.

Lee Roy Parnell

I started out even. It took me 30 years to get five million in debt.

Merle Haggard

Any game you play, you got to lose somtime.

Roy Acuff

Acuff was an unsuccessful candidate for Governor of Tennessee twice in the 1940's.

Sometimes the good Lord has to hit us with a sledgehammer to knock some sense into our heads.

George Jones

You learn the most from life's hardest knocks.

Conway Twitty

Show business is made up of disappointments,
and it's through life's disappointments
that you grow.

Minnie Pearl

If I hadn't had the hurdles along the way,
I wouldn't fully appreciate my success.

Tammy Wynette

Put your trust in the Lord and go ahead.
Worry gets you no place.

Roy Acuff

When I started counting my blessings,
my whole life turned around.

Willie Nelson

If you want the rainbow,
you've got to put up with
a little rain.

Dolly Parton

There ain't nothing that's gonna happen today that me and the Good Lord can't handle.

Plaque on Roy Acuff's wall

5

Change

Fame is fickle and time relentless. Today's stars are tomorrow's old-timers. This fact does not go unnoticed by country's best and brightest. Each took someone else's place on stage, and each must someday relinquish the spotlight to a fresh crop of new talent.

Even country music cannot escape life's eternal constant — change. Here's what the stars have to say about it.

Change is both terrifying and inevitable.

Joe Dittrich

Change is the one thing we can be sure of.

Naomi Judd

Capitalize on change.

Conway Twitty

If you're going to move, you've got to move while you can.

Dolly Parton

A dead end street is a good place to turn around.

Naomi Judd

Success is about evolution. Change is healthy.
I like to reinvent myself.

Faith Hill

Once you become predictable,
no one's interested anymore.

Chet Atkins

When you sit on something trying to
preserve it, you die and become sterile.

Garth Brooks

This business is always changing. If you're
going to be a leader, you've go to take chances.

Ronnie Milsap

You've got to continue to grow, or you're just like last night's cornbread — stale and dry.

Loretta Lynn

Live fast.

Faron Young

Any time you make a change, you're gonna upset some people; but that doesn't mean you don't change. It just means that some people won't like it.

Porter Wagoner

Part of my evolution has been finding my style and finding my voice. Hopefully I'll never stop growing and learning.

Martina McBride

It hurts to be ahead of your time.

Susan Longacre

God has a timetable when the
     seemingly miraculous happens.

Cliffie Stone

Once you replace negative thoughts
     with positive ones, you'll start having
     positive results.

Willie Nelson

The Bible says, "All things are possible."
     I believe that.

Dolly Parton

6

The Performance

Shakespeare, in his wisdom, recognized that "All the world's a stage, and all the men and women merely players." His words still have meaning for all of us.

We are *all* performers. Whether our stage is home, office, church or school, each of us is called upon to do his part. Here are some helpful tips for giving the performance of a lifetime.

If you can't do it with feeling, don't.

Patsy Cline

If you ain't lived it, there ain't no use
in singin' it.

Sammy Kershaw

When the performance is right and the
audience is excited, I'm sixteen again.

Carl Perkins

Once you've gotten used to performing,
you can't give it up.

Minnie Pearl

My stage is my sanctuary...it's the only
place on this earth that I'm in control.

Trace Adkins

Turn loose and have fun.
　　Give the audience a show.
Roy Acuff

It's all about having fun, because fun
　　is why people go to concerts.
Ricky Van Shelton

It's funny how a chubby kid can just be
having fun, and people call it entertainment.
Garth Brooks

I have so much fun on stage that
　　I should have to pay to get in.
Marty Robbins

It's wonderful making records, but there's nothing like walking out on that stage.

Ronnie Dunn

I'm trying to sell every audience something;
that something is me.

Eddy Arnold

I think a singer has to be
a three-minute actor.

Garth Brooks

I'm trying to create high energy on stage.

Shania Twain

Talent is being able to please people.

Marty Robbins

I want 'em to leave liking me.

Tennessee Ernie Ford

Love the audience and they'll love you back.

George D. Hay

This advice was given to a young Minnie Pearl as she nervously awaited her first Opry performance.

Find your own style.

> *Mother's advice to Reba McEntire*

You're not going to succeed if you're
a carbon copy.

> *Roy Acuff*

People ask me where I got my singing style.
I didn't copy my style from anybody.

> *Elvis Presley*

I never wanted to copy any man.

> *Bill Monroe*

I was a pretty good imitator of Roy Acuff, but then I found out they already had a Roy Acuff, so I started singin' like myself.

Hank Williams, Sr.

K now yourself — and your audience.

Tennessee Ernie Ford

G et out on the stage of life.

Cliffie Stone

T here's nobody else like you.

Tandy Rice

M y parents impressed upon me the need
to be creative and take risks. Every night
when I go out on stage, I think about that.

Deana Carter

7

The Road

Country entertainers are intensely aware of travel. Life on the road means year after grinding year of buses, hotels and early morning wake-up calls. Ernest Tubb, for example, still played over 200 engagements a year, long after the social security checks started rolling in. Tubb understood the importance of reaching out to his fans, and he was willing to make the sacrifices necessary to do so.

Here's a brief guided tour of "the road" from men and women who know it all too well. The words on the following pages remind us that the business of making country music is not only a lot of fun — it's also a lot of hard work.

The bus is probably the most important
instrument in country music.

Barbara Mandrell

I spend so much time in a bus it's hard to get
a sense of what's going on in the real world.

Tim McGraw

Finding a good bus driver can be as important
as finding a good musician.

Reba McEntire

When I started, there were no buses or planes.
We did 200 dates a year, averaged 100,000 miles,
and still had to be back in Nashville
every Saturday night for the Opry.
Now that was hard traveling.

Ernest Tubb

Mile after boring mile...

Bill Anderson

In the beginning, if I made enough on a show,
I could get a fifty-cent room. Otherwise,
I slept at the train station.

Chet Atkins

Just starting out, we slept in the back of the car
and lived on baloney and cheese sandwiches.

Loretta Lynn

We did ninety one-nighters in ninety days.
We came home in a box.

Billy Joe Royal

I worked 27 years of one-nighters.

Minnie Pearl

It's a shame that it takes so long on the road
to have those few incredible minutes
with the audience.

Don Williams

Touring is really a pretty lonely business.

Eddy Arnold

I've spent my life on the road.

Mel Tillis

After you ride the bus a hundred zillion
miles and you've been everywhere,
it's good to be home.

Alan Jackson

What I dislike most is the traveling.

Jim Reeves

These words were spoken shortly before Reeves lost his life in an airplane crash.

Playing the road is like robbing Wells Fargo.
You ride in, take the money, and ride out.

Marty Robbins

To say that my fist tour was a financial
disaster would be like saying that the burning
of Atlanta was a nice little bonfire.

Bill Anderson

It's hard to make money on the road,
no matter who you are.

Willie Nelson

I can't sleep in a bed that's not moving.

Tracy Lawrence

8

Work

Playing country music is hard work. The hours are long; the travel is exhausting; and the pay can be slim. Why do so many talented people willingly struggle against such long odds in a business that has a thousand misses for every hit? It's the performers' love for their music.

Whether or not you ever pick up a guitar or microphone, the following words still apply to you and to your life's work. If you take this advice to heart, you will have fun, work hard, and enjoy the music while it plays.

Love what you do or do something else.

Conway Twitty

God respects you when you work,
but He loves you when you sing.

Cliffie Stone

Stay busy and take care of your own business.

Eddy Arnold

Find your inspiration and hone in on it.

Susan Longacre

You shape your own destiny.

Chet Atkins

In Nashville, as in every other city,
there's no substitute for hard work.

Bill Monroe

God has a plan for all of us, but He expects us
to do our share of the work.

Minnie Pearl

When young people ask me how I made it,
I say, "It's absolutely hard work. Nobody's
gonna' wave a magic wand."

Loretta Lynn

Be different, stand out,
and work your butt off.

Reba McEntire

Work for the fun of it, and the money
will arrive someday.

Ronnie Milsap

Don't just work for a paycheck.

Tim DuBois

If I weren't doing it for a living,
I'd be doin' it for fun.

Ricky Van Shelton

I don't do this for the money. My dad still
asks me when I'm going to get a real job.

Ray Stevens

Work is both my living and my pleasure.

Harlan Howard

Nobody's gonna' live for you.

Dolly Parton

Spend your life doing something you believe in.

Charlie Daniels

It's important to keep your dreams alive.

Conway Twitty

When you stop dreaming, you stop living.

Lorrie Morgan

How are you going to make a dream come true
if you don't have one?

Cliffie Stone

You've got to have faith. Think to yourself,
"I'm gonna fight the good fight and win."

Ricky Skaggs

You get to a point where you say, "We're either
going to cut bait and run, or we're going to try to
build something." Build something.

Pam Tillis

You learn how to do good work by being
honest with yourself.

Rodney Crowell

If you do it for the money, you're doing it
for the wrong reasons.

Waylon Jennings

You can't do good work if you're just going
through the motions. You've got to enjoy
what you are doing.

Rick Nelson

You don't do this kind of work for the money.
You do it because you love the music
and the life-style.

Mark Chesnutt

Just give it the best you've got.
Grin and bear it and have a good time.

Alan Jackson

Do the best you can with yourself
and hope for the best.

Loretta Lynn

God was generous enough to give me a talent
and the ambition to use it.

Tammy Wynette

I just keep working hard, keep playing lots of
dates, keep trying to get up to that next level
and see where it goes from there.

Sammy Kershaw

If you're not having fun, you're not doing your job right.

"Cowboy" Jack Clement

9

The Songs

What is a hit song? Bill Anderson believes, "It's a magical little something that you search and search for, and, if you're lucky, you find it once in a lifetime."

What follows are important observations about the very foundation of country music: the song. And you don't have to be Garth Brooks or Patsy Cline to benefit from the advice.

Even if you can't carry a tune in a gunny sack, keep searching for your own "magical little something." Whether you're at work, at home, or at play, your song can be translated through a smile, a prayer or a simple act of kindness. So do yourself — and the rest of us — a big favor: Put a song in your heart and make your own joyful noise. If you do, then your song, no matter what form it takes, is destined to be a hit.

It's not the singer; it's the song.

Conway Twitty

My career has been built with the songs
I write.

Dolly Parton

All of country music goes back to good songs.
Without good songs, we are nothing.

Marty Stuart

Really great songs are few and far between.

Alan Jackson

If you hear something you like and you're
halfway like the public, chances are
they'll like it too.

Chet Atkins

I just try to have fun with it and pick songs
and write songs that I like.

Alan Jackson

A song has to move me before I can sing it.

Faith Hill

I sing the songs I would buy.

Marty Robbins

If you don't feel it, forget it.

Waylon Jennings

Feelings — that's what songs should be about.

Hank Williams, Sr.

Talk about the paths to the heart.

Susan Longacre

It's easy to find a good song, but it's hard
to find a great song.

Tommy Cash

I go through a thousand songs to find ten
for a new record.

Conway Twitty

Taking care of music isn't hard. What's hard
is finding music worth taking care of.

Jimmy Bowen

A song ain't nothin' in the world but a story just wrote with music to it.

Hank Williams, Sr.

People want lyrics that pertain to their lives and to their feelings. I want to write songs that mean something to the audience.

Vince Gill

A song is a poem set to music.

Tom T. Hall

I take a whole story and compress it into three minutes.

Harlan Howard

I hate that song.

Patsy Cline

Her first reaction to the Cochran/Howard classic "I Fall to Pieces"

Nobody knows a hit before it's a hit.

Tom T. Hall

There is no specific formula. The only thing that creates a hit is whether or not it clicks with the audience.

Travis Tritt

I wrote *Happy Trails* in two hours. People liked it, and noboby on earth was more surprised than I was.

Dale Evans

You can change the name of an old song,
rearrange it and make it swing.

Bob Wills

Songs are like jokes; there's not an original
one anywhere.

Archie Campbell

No matter how you slice it, it's just
the same 12 notes.

Charlie Daniels

There are only so many notes, so when
someone does something different with them,
it really impresses you. It doesn't happen
very often.

Kim Richey

Make your melodies simple enough so that the average person can hum them.

Tom T. Hall

Some days you write great, and some days you don't.

Randy Travis

Sometimes a song works and sometimes it doesn't. Either way, don't worry too much. Just keep writing.

Harlan Howard

Everyone has a song in him.

Cliffie Stone

You never know where you'll find a hit.

Faron Young

<u>10</u>

The Songwriters

Songwriters have a special place in the world of country music. These men and women craft the musical mini-dramas that keep fans coming back for more.

The best country songs are deceptively simple; this simplicity masks a fact that seasoned songwriters know all too well: It's incredibly difficult to write a great country song. In fact, many talented composers labor for years before they finally begin to master the many subtleties of their craft.

Great songwriters, like great songs, are few and far between. Here are some observations about songwriting from the people who know.

The Songwriters

It's seldom easy to find your first hit song.
Your best bet is to write it yourself.

Buck Owens

People getting into the business ask me
for advice: I always encourage them to try
to write their own material.

John Anderson

Writing songs has helped my career
more than anything else.

Alan Jackson

When I'm inspired, I get excited because
I can't wait to see what I'll come up with next.

Dolly Parton

I started writing music because I got tired of
looking in the bottom drawer for material
after everyone else had turned it down. It was
like picking out your cleanest dirty shirt.

Vern Gosdin

L.A. is a musician's town.
New York is a lawyer's town.
Nashville is a
songwriter's town.

Bob McDill

The best place to start is with a good title.
Then build a song around it.

Fred Rose

I usually start with a title or maybe
a little rhyme or phrase.

Harlan Howard

Construct a song to reach a climax
at a certain point.

Buddy Killen

Songwriting is as much a craft as a talent.

Tom T. Hall

A big part of writing is listening.
Listen to people talk.

Don Schlitz

I write like I talk.

Roger Miller

I write about things I know: depression, guilt, despair, failed relationships. Everybody has moments of despair; it's just that I exploit mine.

Mary-Chapin Carpenter

When I started, I wrote about hate and bitterness. Eventually, I threw those songs away, but the experience was better than a psychiatrist and a whole lot cheaper.

Jan Howard

My songwriting success? It's just a sense of humor and a good outlook on life.

Roger Miller

I'm trying to put the ache in the music.

Susan Longacre

Country music is about consequences.

Radney Foster

I'm always collecting emotions
for future reference.

Harlan Howard

Write from the heart, not the head.

Mark Miller

If a song can't be written in 20 minutes,
it ain't worth writing.

Hank Williams, Sr.

The great songs just come out.
If it comes quick, just leave it that way.

Marty Robbins

Sometimes the best songs
almost write themselves.

Bill Anderson

I didn't choose a word or anything.
I just wrote the song until it stopped.

Marty Robbins

Describing the experience of writing the song "El Paso City"

I write anywhere, anytime.
I'm open 24 hours a day.

Hal Ketchem

I could no more not write than not breathe.

Kris Kristofferson

If I go a day without writing, it's like a smoker
going a day without a cigarette.

Nanci Griffith

I like myself better when I'm writing regularly.

Willie Nelson

I can't stop writing songs. I still write
like I'm hungry.

Dolly Parton

You've got three minutes to tell a complete story.
Go for simplicity.

Sonny James

You've got three minutes to tell the world
something, so grab their hearts
and say "Listen!"

Garth Brooks

I try to find songs that hit me over the head
and strike a chord in my heart.

Wynonna Judd

A lot of songs you write are just
for exercise — just pencil sharpeners.

Harlan Howard

Part of learning what to write is learning
what to leave out.

Guy Clark

Remember, vanilla still outsells
the other 31 flavors.

Owen Bradley

Being a professional
songwriter beats the heck
out of working.

Harlan Howard

11

The Music Business

The music business is just like any other business, only more so — more ups, more downs, more highs and more lows.

The advice in this chapter will help you make a better showing in *your* competitive world. By following the following advice, you'll become a better producer — whether you're producing records, widgets or sales.

You can't take the music business personally.

Connie Smith

It's a bridge-burning proposition to seek
your fortune in the music business.

Wayland Holyfield

I looked up, and the buzzards were circling
my career.

Roger Miller

You have to have endurance to be
in this business.

Patsy Montana

The music business is strictly business.

Kenny Rogers

Show business was my life until I started
making my living at it.

Jeannie Seely

It's the most unglamourous business
in the world.

Minnie Pearl

Before I had a record deal, I didn't have
much of a glamour life, and now,
it's pretty much the same.

Mary-Chapin Carpenter

Fame is an occupational hazard.

Rosanne Cash

The glamour, the image:
These are things that
I can truly say are
only make believe.

Conway Twitty

It is important to be able to carry a guitar case in one hand and a briefcase in the other.

Travis Tritt

I figure if God gave me this talent, He also meant for me to use good sense with it; and that means good business sense.

Dolly Parton

Sometimes it's like you're a big pie settin'
on the table, and everybody runs up and
gets their piece of you. When it's over,
the plate's empty.

Loretta Lynn

Some of the people I worked with —
I wouldn't say they were crooks, but they
definitely weren't honest.

Vern Gosdin

A long apprenticeship is the most logical way to success. The alternative is overnight stardom, but I can't give you a formula for that.

Chet Atkins

Everybody plays in joints for ten years. That's just learning your trade.

Vince Gill

Practive every time you get a chance.

Bill Monroe

They say love will find a way.
    I know determination will.

Ronnie Milsap

I never gave up on country music because
    I knew what I was doing was not that bad.

Willie Nelson

Just keep pickin', and, if you have enough
    talent, somebody will discover it.

Merle Travis

More than anything, Garth Brooks
taught me that every fan is important.

Ty England

Never forget that the American audience
is essentially moral and sentimental.

Eddy Arnold

You can't cheat the public for long.

Tennessee Ernie Ford

Image is a fragile thing.

Conway Twitty

I don't chase trends. The only time a trend is worth anything is when you create it yourself.

Jimmy Bowen

Fads are the kiss of death. When the fad goes away, you go with it.

Conway Twitty

The trends? They're just a different twist on how to say, "I love you."

Eddy Arnold

I was determined to carve out a music
of my own. I didn't want to copy anybody.

Bill Monroe

I always took a great deal of pride
in being original.

Roger Miller

Don't be a blueprint. Be an original.

Roy Acuff

When I leave this business, it will be
with my hands folded, lying in a box.

Porter Wagoner

The music business? I wouldn't do
anything else. I had a lot of other jobs,
and I hated them all.

Ernest Tubb

12

Stars Talk About Themselves

Many country music stars come from humble beginnings. Given their backgrounds, it's not surprising that these men and women are usually down-to-earth, easy-to-know people. Perhaps this fact helps explain why country fans are so intensely loyal: their favorite stars are also "good ole' boys" — and girls.

Here are some refreshing words from a collection of stars who don't take themselves too seriously. Thank goodness.

I can play a thousand songs and fiddle the bugs off a tater vine.

Uncle Jimmy Thompson

Thomspon was the first performer on "The Tennessee Barn Dance," the radio program which was later renamed "The Grand Ole Opry."

I'm not a major talent, I'm a product
of the people.

Garth Brooks

I don't claim to be a great singer,
by any means. If I can get by with being
an average singer, I'm happy with that.

Tim McGraw

I think I reach people because I'm with them,
not apart from them.

Loretta Lynn

Long before I was a star, I was a fan.

Bill Anderson

I feel like I fell into the luck bucket.

Pam Tillis

I don't know how I lasted.

Minnie Pearl

We were always a little mystified why
forty million people would watch Louise,
Irlene and me cavorting around on stage.

Barbara Mandrell

I was the first singin' cowboy...
maybe not the best. But being "the best"
doesn't matter if you're "the first."

Gene Autry

I can read music, but not enough to hurt my pickin'.

Glen Campbell

Everything I've ever done was out of fear
of being mediocre.

Chet Atkins

Whenever I finish something, I always ask
myself, "Well, Stutterin' Boy,
is that all you got?"

Mel Tillis

I never had a doubt in my mind. I always knew that, with the right material, I could pop a hit.

Kenny Rogers

Even as a kid working in a cotton patch and living in shotgun houses, I knew something was gonna' happen. I just knew it.

Conway Twitty

When I stepped out on the stage of the Opry, it was like stepping into a picture I'd been looking at all my life.

Clint Black

I was born to live in Nashville.

Harlan Howard

Most of the stuff I've read about me has been true.

Willie Nelson

I don't think my music will ever venture
too far from what I've always done.
Country music is just what I do.

Alan Jackson

There's the guy I'd love to be, and the guy I am.
I'm somewhere in between.

Merle Haggard

I tend to average about 10 hit songs per ex-wife.

Vern Gosdin

I'll never live to see thirty.

Patsy Cline

Spoken to Dottie West — Cline died in a plane crash at age 30.

I'll Never Get Out of This World Alive.

The title of the Hank Williams song that
was on the charts at the time of his death

I want my music to leave an indelible mark.

Roger Miller

I'd rather try everything and regret a few things rather than do nothing.

Dolly Parton

I just want to see everybody live and be happy. Me included.

George Jones

Along the way, I learned that hard times can also be good times. If I could live my hard times over again, I would.

Bill Monroe

Looking back on it, I wouldn't change a thing.

Tennessee Ernie Ford

13

Observations on Love, Work, Family, Iced Tea, and Other Necessities of Life

We conclude with some fun, some truth, and some encouragement from members of the country music family.

Home life is everything.

Alan Jackson

Whoever said you can't go home again
wasn't from Yukon, Oklahoma.

Garth Brooks

You don't have to be of the same gender
to be a chip off the old block.

Barbara Mandrell

Hope is a gift we give ourselves, and it remains when all else is gone.

Naomi Judd

Pain comes like the
weather, but joy
is a choice.

Rodney Crowell

I ain't worried about dying.
I'm worried about living.

Doug Stone

Every day is a good day to be alive,
whether the sun's shining or not.

Marty Robbins

As a kid, my dad taught me this:
You'd better be thankful for what you've got!

Garth Brooks

Time is one of my most valuable assets.

Bill Anderson

The greatest conflicts are not between
two people but between one person
and himself.

Garth Brooks

Where you lose it first is between the ears.

Conway Twitty

One of the greatest unknowns
is inside the mind.

Lee Roy Parnell

Your body hears everything your mind says.

Naomi Judd

When they say it can't be done, remember that it can.

Col. Tom Parker

It's one thing to have talent. It's another
to figure out how to use it.

Roger Miller

Your talent is God's gift to you.
How you use it is your gift to God.

Country Saying

There are many paths but only one journey.

Naomi Judd

Life is an individual sport. And life is a team
sport. I love those two statements. And even
though they contradict each other,
they're both right.

Garth Brooks

Life ain't a dress rehearsal.

Waylon Jennings

I've learned you can recover from a wrong
turn. And even if life doesn't turn out according
to expectations, it's okay to be yourself.

Faith Hill

I think it made a better person out of me
to go through the highs and lows,
the peaks and valleys.

Tammy Wynette

Growing up is not being so dead-set
on making everybody happy.

Reba McEntire

I don't want to be "middle of the road."
The only things in the middle of the road are
white lines and dead possums.

Billy Ray Cyrus

Divorces, split-ups, extra boyfriends and girlfriends: I don't know where people find the time.

Loretta Lynn

Three classic mistakes are choosing the wrong religion, dabbling in politics, and hurting people.

Tom T. Hall

One thing I've always enjoyed is foolin' with a garden. Home-grown vegetables keep us down to earth.

John Anderson

Iced tea is only good if the sugar is put in when it is made.

Hank Williams, Jr.

Being a star means that you just find your own special place and shine right where you are.

Dolly Parton

Sources

Roy Acuff: Singer, Songwriter, Emcee, "The King of
  Country Music" 22, 49, 50, 64, 68, 125
Trace Adkins: Singer, Songwriter 63
Bill Anderson: Singer, Songwriter, TV Personality 73, 77,
  108, 129, 143
John Anderson: Singer, Songwriter 49, 102
Eddy Arnold: Singer, Songwriter, TV Personality, "The
  Tennessee Plowboy" 17, 22, 66, 75, 81, 122, 124
Chet Atkins: Guitarist, Composer, Recording Industry
  Executive 18, 46, 48, 56, 74, 81, 93, 120, 132
Gene Autry: "Singing Cowboy," Actor 130
Clint Black: Singer, Songwriter 32, 133
Jimmy Bowen: Recording Industry Executive, Producer
  95, 124
Owen Bradley: Recording Industry Executive, Producer
  111
Garth Brooks: Singer, Songwriter 17, 20, 30, 32, 40, 56, 64,
  66, 91, 110, 129, 140, 144, 143, 146
George Bush: United States President 31
Archie Campbell: Comedian 98
Glen Campbell: Singer, Studio Musician 131
Mary-Chapin Carpenter: Singer, Songwriter 106, 116
Deana Carter: Singer, Songwriter 70
Johnny Cash: Singer, Songwriter 25
Rosanne Cash: Singer, Songwriter 116
Tommy Cash: Singer, Songwriter 95
Mark Chesnutt: Singer, Songwriter 88
Guy Clark: Singer, Songwriter 111
Terri Clark: Singer, Songwriter 41
Jack Clement: Producer 90
Patsy Cline: Singer, Songwriter 62, 91, 97, 136
Jerry Clower: Comedian 18
Floyd Cramer: Pianist, Songwriter 34

Sources

Waylon Jennings: Singer, Songwriter 20, 88, 94, 147

George Jones: Singer, Songwriter 49, 137

Naomi Judd: Singer, Songwriter, Author 46, 54, 55, 141, 144, 146

Wynonna Judd: Singer 110

Sammy Kershaw: Singer, Songwriter 38, 63, 89

Hal Ketchem: Singer, Songwriter 109

Buddy Killen: Music Industry Executive, Insrumentalist, Songwriter, Author 104

Kris Kristofferson: Singer, Songwriter, Actor 109

Tracy Lawrence: Singer, Songwriter 78

Don Light: Talent Agent 21

Susan Longacre: Songwriter 59, 81, 94, 107

Loretta Lynn: Singer, Songwriter, Author 38, 46, 48, 57, 74, 82, 89, 119, 129, 149

Barbara Mandrell: Singer, Songwriter, Television Personality, Author 72, 130, 140

Kathy Mattea: Singer, Songwriter 24

Martina McBride: Singer, Songwriter 59

Bob McDill: Songwriter 103

Ronnie Dunn: Singer, Songwriter 65

Jackie McEntire: Reba's Mother 68

Reba McEntire: Singer, Songwriter 72, 83, 148

Tim McGraw: Singer, Songwriter 72, 129

Mark Miller: Singer, Songwriter, Member of Sawyer Brown 107

Roger Miller: Singer, Songwriter 105, 106, 115, 125, 137, 146

Ronnie Milsap: Singer, Songwriter, Pianist 16, 34, 56, 84, 121

Bill Monroe: Singer, Songwriter, Instrumentalist, "Father of Bluegrass" 31, 33, 68, 82, 120, 125, 137

Patsy Montana: Singer, Songwriter 115

Ricky Skaggs: Singer, Songwriter, Instrumentalist 87

Connie Smith: Singer, Songwriter 114

Ray Stevens: Singer, Songwriter 84

Cliffie Stone: Music Industry Executive, Songwriter, Singer, Author 60, 70, 81, 87, 99

Doug Stone: Singer, Songwriter 17, 37, 143

Marty Stuart: Singer, Songwriter 92

Uncle Jimmy Thompson: Fiddler 128

Sonny Throckmorton: Songwriter, Singer 23, 24

Mel Tillis: Singer, Songwriter, Music Industry Executive 40, 75, 132

Pam Tillis: Singer, Songwriter, Daughter of Mel Tillis 31, 34, 40, 87, 130

Merle Travis: Singer, Songwriter, Guitarist 121

Randy Travis: Singer, Songwriter 99

Travis Tritt: Singer, Songwriter 97, 118

Ernest Tubb: Singer, Songwriter, Actor 28, 71, 72, 126

Shania Twain: Singer, Songwriter 38, 66

Conway Twitty: Singer, Songwriter, Actor 23, 29, 32, 49, 54, 80, 87, 92, 95, 117, 123, 124, 133, 144

Ricky Van Shelton: Singer, Songwriter 64, 84

Porter Wagoner: Singer, Songwriter, Television Personality 34, 59, 126

Don Williams: Singer, Songwriter 13, 75

Hank Williams, Jr.: Singer, Songwriter 40, 149

Hank Williams, Sr.: Singer, Songwriter 13, 15, 30, 69, 94, 96, 108, 136

Bob Wills: Singer, Songwriter, Fiddler, Pioneer of "Western Swing" 98

Tammy Wynette: Singer, Songwriter 50, 89, 148

Trisha Yearwood: Singer, Songwriter 43

Dwight Yoakam: Singer, Songwriter 17, 44

Faron Young: Singer, Songwriter 58, 100